TESTIMO

"Thank you for opening my spirit to new ways to communicate with God."

RICHARD, COLORADO

"Frankly I cannot put in words...I just felt like my chains broke."

TYANNAH, CALIFORNIA

"God showed me how I'm allowed to dream big and play big...that there is no lid on my life."

NOOMI, CALIFORNIA

"I felt everything so deeply. I knew who I must forgive, and when I forgave them it brought so much freedom."

ANONYMOUS, CALIFORNIA

"I enjoyed every step of the process because it's like a personal walk with God for my deepest emotions which I don't normally share with anyone."

SHALLY, CALIFORNIA

"I found a lie that I never thought about and how it's been influencing me. To have Abba talk to me about His viewpoint filled me with hope."

KATY, CALIFORNIA

"I wasn't really expecting God to reveal to me what He did, but it was like a breath of fresh air and lovely to have a visual reminder of how good God is and how personal and intimate His communication with me can be."

LEANNA, NEW ZEALAND

"The Holy Spirit showed me that I had believed the
lie that I didn't matter to Him and that He cannot see me.
He revealed that lie came from childhood/parents missed
opportunities to love. Holy Spirit showed me that He does see me
and want me. He saw me as His righteousness and made in His image.
I'm His treasure and He loves to spend time with me."

VICTORIA, WASHINGTON

"God reminded me of finger painting as a little girl.
He's going to bring me back to that type of freedom."

AMANDA, IDAHO

"God showed me that instead of striving for God's provision,
He has created me with His provision being a part of my identity."

CANDICE, CALIFORNIA

"I was touched by God and heard Him speak to me...
about increasing my peace. Painting sorrow and having
God reveal an enemy plan to deepen my sorrow is very revealing.
Taking the time to paint the layers of the lie and then the truth
and listening for Him to speak and be blessed to hear Him tell
me is very sweet and healing and life giving. It showed how
personal God is and how available."

TAMERA, WASHINGTON

"I could feel a hand on my left shoulder and hear
God say, 'You are one of a kind.'"

MATTHEW, CALIFORNIA

"God showed me the truth of how abundantly He
was there for me during my darkest hour. While I had thought
I was hanging onto Him by a thread, He actually was infusing
life and even new life to me through a stronger connection."

R. A., CALIFORNIA

"I broke through to God."

GWEN, CALIFORNIA

"As I painted, I saw a picture of myself that I never thought was possible for me. A dream that I always considered a pipe dream."

JANESSA, CANADA

"God showed me that I live under the lie that I live under heavy burdens, have to work terribly hard, but am still separated from God my Father. In forgiving my dad and receiving the forgiveness of God the Father, He filled me and transformed with light and joy, clothed me with royal purple and gave me royal gifts, and the darkness was overcome. I am no longer separated from God my Father."

ANONYMOUS, CALIFORNIA

"I believe I will pursue creating with paint. It's something I enjoyed as a child and haven't painted in decades. The Lord is reawakening some artistic ability that's been dormant for way too long."

JEAN, CALIFORNIA

"I always wondered why I struggled hearing Holy Spirit but I know now I was believing a lie that He didn't exist. That is so freeing to let that lie go and know that Holy Spirit is always with me and I can hear Him clearly."

JANET, WASHINGTON

"It's always surprising to see how powerfully emotions come out on a canvas, and to see how the Lord engages me, in my emotions of an experience, and carries me to a new level of trust in Him because of His deep love for me."

SHANNON, CALIFORNIA

"'Jesus as Friend' wrecked me. Just exposing the lie that I can't come until I have figured out my emotions made me feel so sad for myself and lonely. I felt so much freedom as I experienced forgiveness giving me life and giving me permission to come to Jesus as my safe friend, completely open."

HANNAH, CALIFORNIA

"God brought up a lie I didn't recognize I believed,
but as soon as He said it I started to tear up. He walked me
through each piece, reminding me I could rest in Him instead of
trying to 'make it work,' speaking truth that He delighted in me."

KERIANA, IDAHO

"Through the Art Sozo I identified the lie that has held
me down from truly living. The lie that I was rejected by God
and needed to fix myself. Once I identified this lie I better understood
my fears and my habits. I have begun a healing journey."

ANONYMOUS, IDAHO

"It helped me to examine emotions which are
usually suppressed without any trauma producing them."

BRIAN, UNITED KINGDOM

"Interacting with color and emotion allowed me to
access a lie that directly hindered my belief about Holy Spirit.
Getting past the lie and to the revelation that God revealed in truth
gave me another tool to access His truth and love for me."

DREW, OREGON

"God revealed to me that I am afraid He will hurt me and
take away what I love, as my lie. He showed me that He has
good plans for me. He calls me by name and says I am a princess.
That is a new concept for me to be called a princess. Beautiful Father."

KRISTEN, IDAHO

"I got to hear from the Lord in a way that I haven't in awhile.
I liked seeing that I can put color with emotion."

LINDSEY, OREGON

CONNECTING TO
God's Heart

ART SOZO

PAINTING WITH GOD

GAIL SPOONER

ART SOZO: PAINTING WITH GOD

Connecting to God's Heart

By Gail Spooner

Cover Painting: Gail Spooner
Copy Editor: Sarah Wind
Editor: Lindsey McCallum
Contributor: Gillian Kingsley
Cover Design & Internal Layout: Jonathan McGraw

DISCLAIMER

The use of this book is intended for encounter art with God. It is not designed to treat depression or other illnesses. Please consult your physician before you decide to go off any medications or change your course of treatment. If you are currently in therapy, please consult with your counselor or mental health professional, before starting these activities. It is your responsibility to care for your heart as you embark on these activities. Please see page 23 for more information.

DEDICATION

This book is dedicated to those who have gone before me in healing journeys, to those who walked beside me in mine, and to those who are pursuing their own healing with God by their side. Each one's courage and dedication is inspiring and changing not only their own life, but the lives of those around them for generations to come. May God bless you as you continue to encounter Him.

ACKNOWLEDGEMENTS

Thank you to the many participants of the Art Sozo Workshop who were willing to encounter God in a new way. You kept alive the dream of spreading this art process to others by your inspiring stories of all God showed you as you encountered Him.

To the students of 3rd year BSSM for participating in the Advanced Ministry Training that piloted these activities. Your feedback and inspiring stories of what God healed in your life made it all the more evident that we needed to get this out for others to experience. Thanks for taking a risk to join us!

To Gillian Kingsley, my 2016-2017 Art Sozo 3rd year intern, your dedication to Art Sozo and to the dream of this book helped make it a reality. Many thanks for your contributions.

A special thank you to Lindsey McCallum, the editor of this book. Her belief in this project and tireless hours of editing has made this book come alive on the page. I am forever grateful for your assistance!

I am so thankful to the Art Sozo Team for your prayers, painting through the activities and giving insight and feedback. Your dedication to the Art Sozo Ministry at Bethel Church has made this ministry possible!

Thank you to Dawna DeSilva, Teresa Liebscher and Yvonne Martinez for your guidance in helping me steward the Art Sozo Ministry.

To my wonderful husband Eli, thank you for walking out this adventure with me. Your insight, wisdom, and encouragement has helped me over hurdles and paved the way smooth for this book to happen. I would not want to be doing this journey with anyone other than you!

To my daughters, Denise and Janelle, you have grown into such beautiful, godly, authentic young women and you inspire me daily. Thank you for your belief in the work God has called me to do, and for your assistance and encouragement. I call you both daughters, as well as friends.

CONTENTS

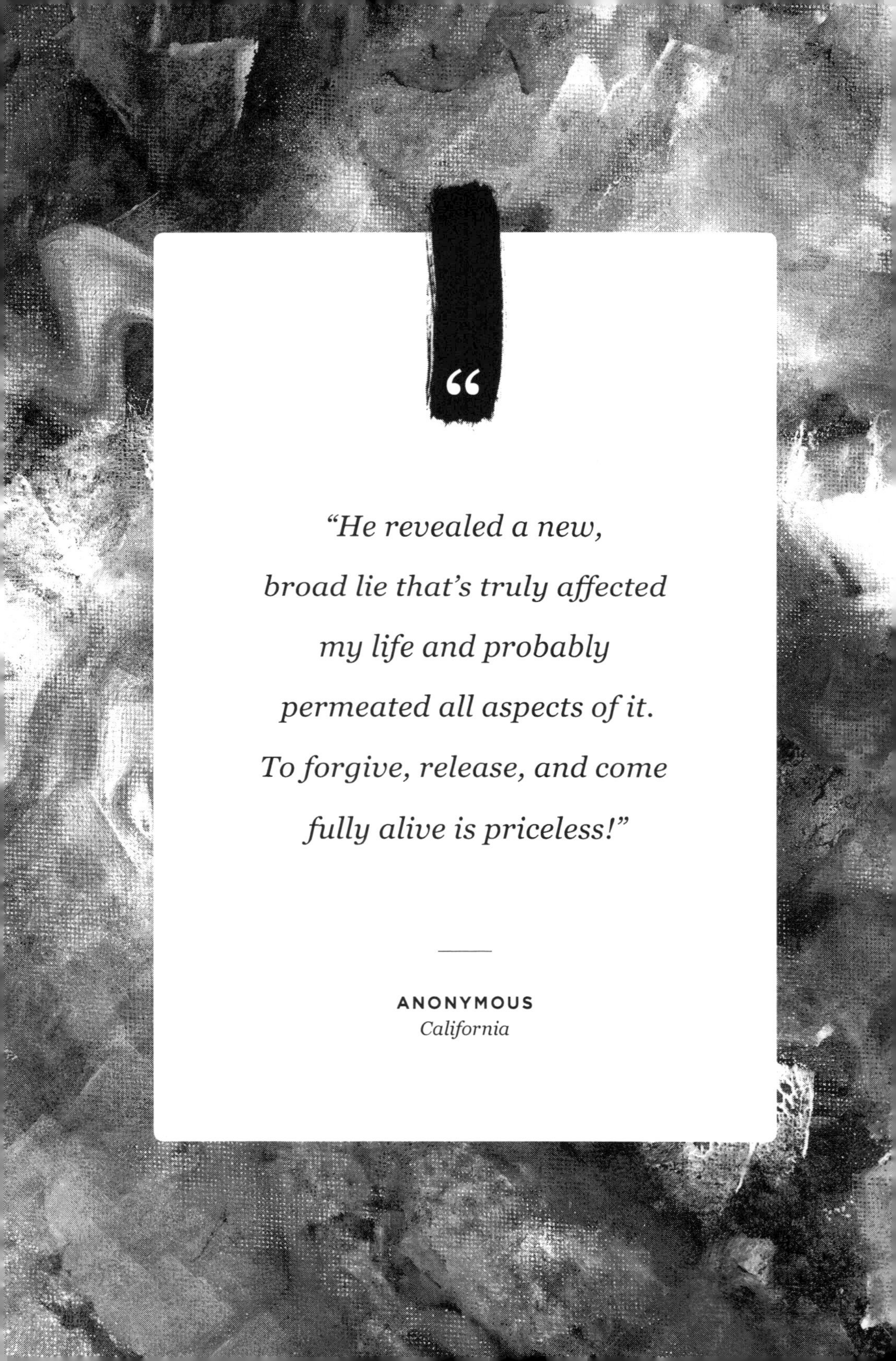

“

“He revealed a new, broad lie that’s truly affected my life and probably permeated all aspects of it. To forgive, release, and come fully alive is priceless!”

ANONYMOUS
California

CHAPTER ONE

INTRODUCTION

Just by picking up this book, you have already put yourself in the way of encounters with God. This book will give you the opportunity to embark on a journey of healing, revelation, and freedom through "encounter art" with our Creator. The goal of Art Sozo is for you to be fully connected to God and His heart for you, without the hindrance of wounds and lies getting in the way and clouding the truth of who He really is. This will bring more intimacy into your relationship with God as you connect to His heart and experience Him more fully in your life.

Art Sozo: Painting with God, offers you a unique way to encounter God using acrylic paint and journaling. As you express your emotions to God and let Him reveal Himself, you will experience a healing journey. The good news is that fine art skills are not needed, as you will learn the freedom of "encounter art" and the joy of having God reveal truth to you on the canvas. It is less about the end product and more about the process of your heart being healed as you paint, bringing freedom, breakthrough, and lasting connection with God.

You will encounter the true nature of Father God as your Protector, Provider, and the One who calls out your identity. You will have the opportunity to experience Holy Spirit as your Counselor, Nurturer, and Comforter. The activities will take you through encounters with Jesus as your Savior, Companion, and Friend. Each activity is designed to take about 45 minutes to complete, though you may take as much time as feels comfortable for you. Once completed, you will have a visual reminder of the truth God has shown you.

The purpose of each Art Sozo activity is to reveal wounds and lies that have resulted in a false perception of God or yourself, guide you in the process of forgiveness for those responsible, and empower you to let go of any false beliefs that don't align with God's truth.[1] Through these activities many are able to break through in areas they have felt stuck, feeling a renewed sense of joy, freedom, and creativity. This approach to inner healing is powerful because it invites God to touch our emotions in a tangible way through art.

Art Sozo invites you to surrender any limiting assumptions about yourself or your artistic skills in order to co-create with God. He loves when we are open to partnering with Him and simply wants us to enjoy the creative process.

"For we are God's masterpiece. He has created us anew in Christ Jesus, so we can do the good things he planned for us long ago" Ephesians 2:10 (NLT).

In the co-creating process of your Art Sozo journey, God is able to speak to any issue He highlights and bring healing, often with just one stroke of paint. This process is both physical and spiritual. Painting activates the limbic system of the brain. This is your "emotional brain," and the movement of painting allows emotions to rise up that may normally be suppressed by your logical defenses. God brings truth and healing into these areas through forgiveness. Forgiveness is foundational; it is the key to unlock the healing of the heart.

GAIL'S STORY

Art Sozo is the result of my own emotional healing journey. Growing up in a home where negative emotions were not allowed, I learned to push my feelings down rather than process them. As I got older, my emotions manifested as physical pain in my body. I often would not know I was upset about something until my jaw would tighten up or I'd get a stomach ache. My emotions were desperate to get out and no longer be bottled up and I had no idea how to process them.

1: "But how could I believe a lie about God?" Please refer to Appendix A - "Common Questions" for answers to this and other questions that may come up.

A friend asked me if I wanted to come to her studio and try to paint my emotions. Anger and sadness poured out of me onto the canvas, because it was a safe place to release the pain I had buried. As I was painting, I would pray and ask God, "What do You want me to know about this situation?" I would paint over the pain with what God said was true. Each picture had some sort of redemption to it, and from that day on, I had a new way to stay connected to my emotions, and process things that came up in my life. I call this type of art, "encounter art," since it truly is an encounter time with God, our Creator.

After receiving Sozo ministry, which revealed and addressed the root of my core issues, I realized that combining the Sozo inner healing tools with the encounter art I had found to be so healing would be powerful in helping others find breakthrough and healing as well. Upon completing an internship at Bethel Church in the Transformation Center with Dawna DeSilva and Teresa Liebscher, my dream to create an inner healing art ministry came true in the form of the Art Sozo Workshop.[2]

I love helping others encounter God and find inner healing through Art Sozo. My team and I have seen God touch many lives in powerful ways in the workshops. So much so, I want to make sure everyone has access to the Art Sozo process themselves. This activity book is designed to give individuals an opportunity to experience the Art Sozo process on their own at home and for participants of the Art Sozo Workshop to continue their Art Sozo healing journey.

I believe in Sozo as a way of life, a continual process of being fully connected to your own emotions as well as fully connecting to God for His truth. This book is an invitation for you to join us on this journey of inner healing and intimacy with God. My hope is you will be inspired to use it as a guide into freedom of expression and lasting connection to the heart of God.

2: Refer to "The Art Sozo Workshop" in Appendix B.

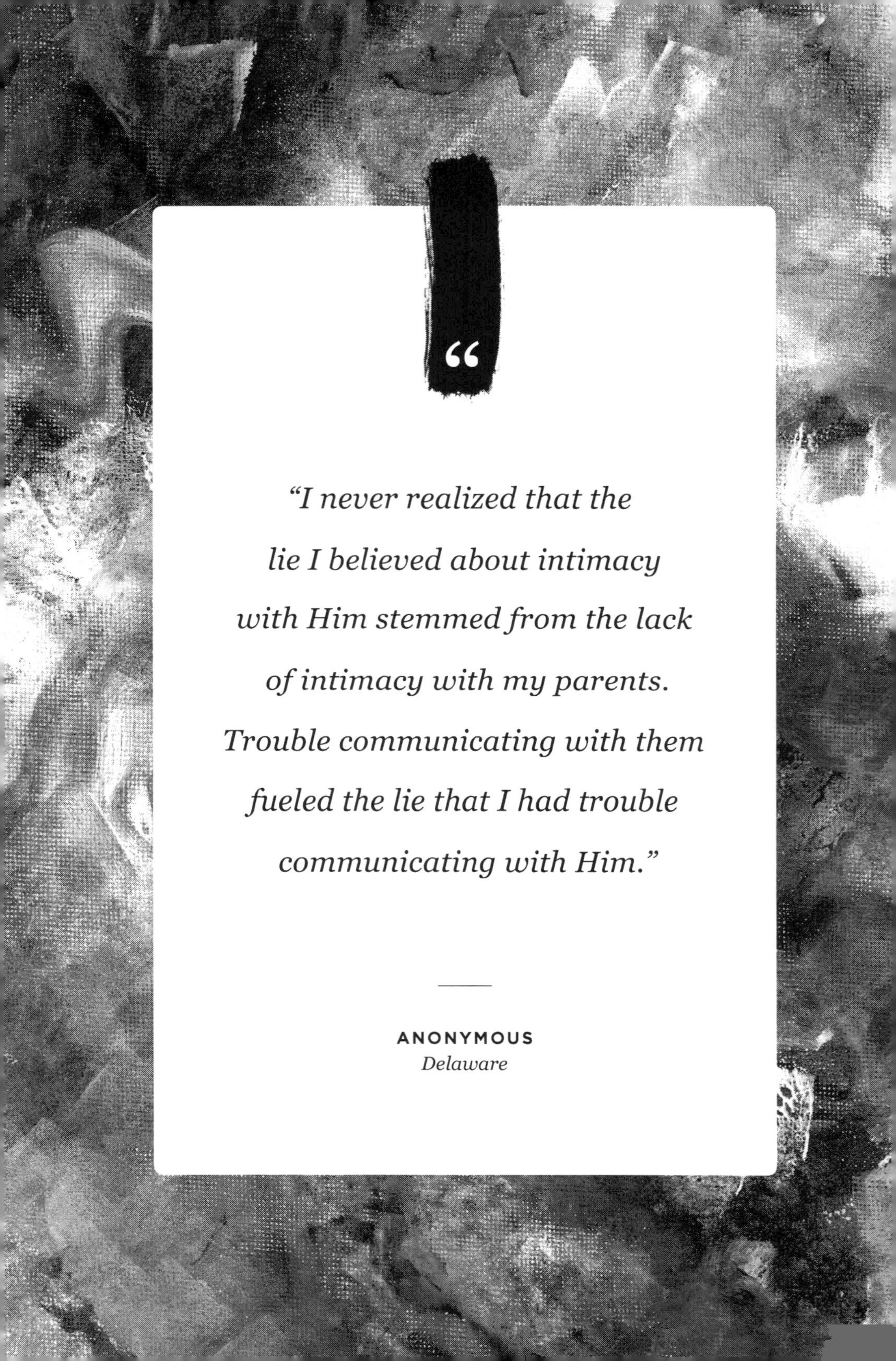

"I never realized that the lie I believed about intimacy with Him stemmed from the lack of intimacy with my parents. Trouble communicating with them fueled the lie that I had trouble communicating with Him."

ANONYMOUS
Delaware

CHAPTER TWO

UNDERSTANDING THE ART SOZO PROCESS

Art Sozo is a combination of encounter art and Bethel Sozo inner healing tools.[1] In this activity book, you will encounter the three Persons of the Godhead: Father God, Jesus, and Holy Spirit. As humans, we try to understand our infinite God through our own life observations and human relationships, using them as our framework for who He is and who we are in Him. Misunderstandings and hurts can cloud our perception of the truth of who God really is. Here are some ways that different earthly relationships can affect our relationship with God.

Father God

Our relationships with our earthly fathers may affect our ability to know and relate with Father God. Since our earthly fathers are human, they will fail us in one way or another. It can be hard to connect to Father God as a loving, protecting father when this has happened. Whether you had the best daddy in the world or one who hurt your heart, Father God will always exceed your expectations as your perfect heavenly Father.

Jesus

Siblings and friends can cause wounds and lies when we are children. These lies can be projected onto Jesus without us being aware of it as adults, hindering our ability to draw close to Him as our Friend and Companion.

1: The "Father Ladder" Sozo tool used in Art Sozo can be found in the Basic Sozo Training Manual by Dawna De Silva & Teresa Liebscher.

Holy Spirit

Our mothers are our best role model of who Holy Spirit is in our lives. Not everyone has a great experience of comfort, nurturing, and teaching from their mothers. However unintentional they may have been, mother wounds can prevent us from being able to fully receive those vital attributes from Holy Spirit.

The good news is that if we open our hearts to God, He is faithful to highlight the areas of wounds and lies that are distancing us from Him, and to reveal Himself in truth. As you draw near to God and let Him reveal any hurts and painful experiences from the past, He will meet you, and show you His true nature. He is God, perfect in all His ways, and He is always good. He has proven it and will continue to prove it as you surrender to Him.

While you're painting, remember the words of John 3:17: *"God sent his Son into the world not to judge the world, but to save the world through him" (NLT).*

The Greek word for "save" used here is actually "Sozo," which means "to save, make whole, heal."[2] According to this verse and the well-known preceding verse, if our beliefs about our experiences do not lead to love, life, forgiveness, healing, and wholeness, they are not of God. Shame, guilt, and condemnation have no place in God's Kingdom or in our lives because Jesus paid the price on the cross. We have a never ending victory in Jesus!

For more verses on God's nature, please refer to Appendix C - "Verses About the Nature of God."

PAINTING LAYER UPON LAYER

While painting these activities, you will be asking God questions about any lies you are believing about Him.[3] Each question will be answered with a new layer of paint on the canvas as you express a lie, let Him reveal who you may need to forgive, paint the truths He illuminates, and encounter how He feels about

---

2: According to Strong's G4982 entry on BlueLetterBible.com.

3: A lie about God? Please refer to Appendix A - "Common Questions."

you.[4] You will use just two colors on each layer. If you use more, the canvas will have too many colors and the likelihood increases of it becoming brownish black. Paint about 5 minutes during each question. With each layer you may choose to cover up the previous one, swirl through it, or leave each layer distinct. Just follow what God shows and tells you and trust the outcome to Him.

Let go of any assumptions about what you'd like to paint, embrace the process as it unfolds, and let the outcome surprise you. There is no right or wrong way to express your emotions and encounter God through art!

After you've painted an Art Sozo activity, take some time to journal about what God showed you.[5] He will often reveal more of His truth as you process with Him and as you write down what you're hearing and sensing. The finished paintings will carry and keep releasing these truths to you and to others as a testimony of His goodness in your life.

Take each step at your own pace, and listen to God as He encourages you to take time to paint or to even repeat activities. If you ever finish painting and you aren't sensing the nature of God being explored, it might also be an area where a traditional Sozo session would help. Please note that the first nine activities are meant to be done in order before moving on to the rest of the Art Sozo activities. These exercises lay the groundwork for the practice of encountering God through art. The activities after the first nine are more advanced, and a firm foundation is needed to keep your heart safe as you proceed deeper.

This Art Sozo process is repeated throughout the activities, helping you to connect with God, hear His truth, and find healing for your heart at a deeper level as you encounter Him. You will be amazed at the freedom you experience during these painting times!

Enjoy the journey.

4: See information on forgiveness in Appendix A - "Common Questions."

5: See "A Note on Journaling" in Appendix D.

“

“I have painted a long time but quit because perfection made it not fun. This was exhilarating. I painted my spirit. So fun!”

CASSIE
Texas

CHAPTER THREE

PREPARING FOR THE JOURNEY

Every successful journey begins with preparation. This chapter will help you set up your Art Sozo area and understand what supplies you will need to begin.

Art Sozo is about the process of connecting to God, first and foremost. To help you stay connected to your emotions as you paint and express them without concern for how your painting turns out, you will be painting with makeup sponges and cotton swabs instead of paintbrushes. This is by design and will give you freedom to focus on your feelings and what God is showing you on this journey of encounter art with Him. Have fun following His lead and letting Him surprise you with the outcome.

SUPPLIES

You will need the following supplies for each of the 14 activities in this book. For suggestions on where to find the supplies mentioned, please refer to Appendix E - "Recommended Resources."

- Acrylic Paint - red, orange, yellow, green, blue, purple, brown, white, and black
- 1 - 10" disposable foam plate to use as a paint pallet for each painting
- 1 - 7" disposable foam plate to use to mix paints and hold used sponges and cotton swabs for each painting
- Foam wedge sponges (sold as makeup sponges) - about 10 per painting

- Cotton swabs - about 15 per painting
- Pen
- Facial tissues for any emotions that may arise
- Bible
- 8.5" x 11" white copy paper - for the *The 4 Emotions* activity
- Tape
- Apron
- Small cup of water to thin paint, if desired
- Wet wipes for easy clean up of hands and painting area
- Plastic tablecloth
- A music playlist that best facilitates creativity and intimacy with God for you. Music without lyrics is preferred. Music suggestions can be found in Appendix E - "Recommended Resources."
- Motsenbocker's LIFT OFF (acrylic paint remover for clothing, if needed)
- Canvas - suggested size 8" x 10" minimum up to 11" x 14" maximum to avoid warping – 1 per activity. Below are some suggestions for types of canvas you can use:
    - Flat Canvas Panels: Panels are easy to display and frame if you'd like to develop an Art Sozo gallery.
    - Mixed Media Paper Pad: A spiral bound notebook with 98 lb. or heavier paper will create an art journal with your art pieces. Paper will tend to curl as it gets wet paint on it, but lays flat again once each painting dries and the notebook is closed.
    - Acrylic Paper Pad: An art pad of 246 lb. acrylic paper. Each sheet stays flat while painting and is easy to frame. Pages tend to come loose from the glued binding.

SETTING UP YOUR ART SOZO AREA

Choose a peaceful place where you can set up and paint for about 45 minutes without distraction. Use the plastic tablecloth to cover the surface you will be using, and arrange your journal, canvas, pen, tissues, and all other supplies onto your workspace. Silence your cell phone so you will not be disturbed. I do not suggest eating while doing the exercises as it may become a distraction.

CARING FOR YOUR HEART

Throughout this process as you paint with God, emotions may surface that you did not realize you had within you. Should you feel you would like additional support while using this book, I encourage you to schedule a Bethel Sozo session, either in person, over the phone, or over Skype. You may call the Bethel Transformation Center (530-229-7909) to schedule an appointment.

Additionally, *www.bethelsozo.com/sozo-network* lists Bethel Sozo counselors that may be near to you.

If you are not familiar with Bethel Sozo or would like more information about the inner healing Sozo ministry at Bethel Church in Redding, California, please turn to Appendix F - "Bethel Sozo."

If you are already working with a therapist or counselor, let them know you are going to be starting your Art Sozo journey. In that way, they will be fully informed and can give you the emotional support you may need.

If at anytime feelings surface that cause you to want to harm yourself or others, please call your local emergency number immediately. In the United States, call 9-1-1.

“I was overwhelmed when I painted what joy felt like. I feel God opened up my soul wider and poured more joy into me.”

SANDY
Oregon

CHAPTER FOUR

PAINTING YOUR EMOTIONS

You are now ready to take the next step on your Art Sozo journey: putting paint to paper! You will begin with a quick warm-up exercise called *The 4 Emotions*. This exercise will prime the pump before you move on to the Art Sozo activities, and it will help you get used to dipping into the paints and expressing freely.

No matter how many times you do this activity, it will turn out differently according to how you're feeling that day. That's the beauty of it. There is no correct way to express an emotion, so you can just paint and see what happens. You are simply expressing your heart, your inner emotions, onto the paper without evaluation in order to learn the process.

Start by setting out your tablecloth, sponges, cotton swabs, 1 sheet of paper, a pen, a cup of water, and a small 7" plate to mix paint and hold used materials. Use the 10" plate to get your paints ready by squeezing a quarter-sized amount of each color onto the plate (see Appendix G - "Paint Plate Diagram").

Helpful tip: To minimize waste, you can store your paint plate in the refrigerator after painting. After rubbing a little water on the outside rim, use another plate to cover it so that you can reuse it in the future. The paint will stay fresh for about two weeks.

THE 4 EMOTIONS EXERCISE[1]

When you're ready to begin, put on your Art Sozo playlist. "Have Courage" by Justin Byrne from his album *Dreaming in Color* is a wonderful instrumental song for this activity.

Take a piece of 8.5" x 11" white copy paper and fold it in half lengthwise, then again widthwise, so you end up with four boxes. Label the top left corner "Anger," the top right corner "Peace," the bottom left corner "Sadness," and the bottom right corner "Joy."

ART SOZO ENCOUNTER ACTIVITY

Anger

Take a deep breath and relax. Think of the emotion anger. What does anger look like to you? How does it feel? What color is anger to you? When you are ready, pick one color and express this emotion in the top left corner of your paper using a cotton swab or sponge and paint any shape or form that best expresses anger for you. After about one minute, put your painting utensil down.

Peace

Again, take a deep breath and relax. Think of the emotion peace. What does peace look like to you? How does it feel? What color is peace to you? When you are ready, pick one color and express this emotion in the top right corner of your paper using a cotton swab or sponge and paint any shape or form that best expresses peace for you. After about one minute, put your painting utensil down.

1: Used by permission from Laurie Zaigon at Art4Healing (www.art4healing.org).

Sadness

Take another deep breath and relax. Think of the emotion sadness. What does sadness look like to you? How does it feel? What color is sadness to you? When you are ready, pick one color and express this emotion in the bottom left corner of your paper using a cotton swab or sponge and paint any shape or form that best expresses sadness for you. After about one minute, put your painting utensil down.

Joy

Take a deep breath and relax. Think of the emotion joy. What does joy look like to you? How does it feel? What color is joy to you? When you are ready, pick one color and express this emotion in the bottom left corner of your paper using a cotton swab or sponge and paint any shape or form that best expresses joy for you. After about one minute, put your painting utensil down. Your painting is complete.

How are you feeling? Isn't it amazing how you were able to quickly express an emotion with only one color? This same process will be used in the rest of the Art Sozo activities in this book. God's desire is to encounter you as you paint, and all you need to do is show up. It really is that easy.

Use the following pages to journal how you felt and what God showed you while you painted the 4 Emotions.

JOURNAL

JOURNAL

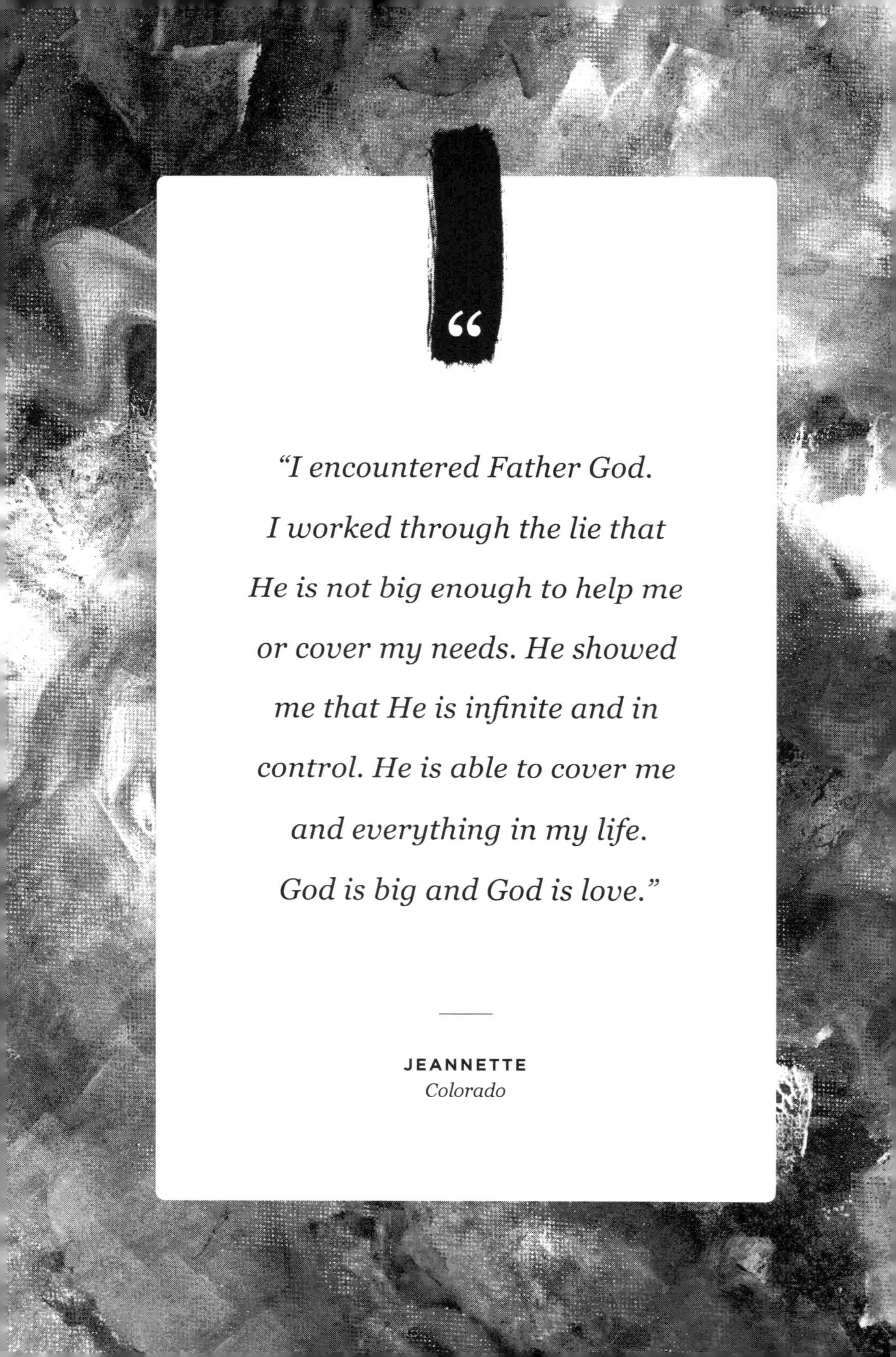

“

“I encountered Father God. I worked through the lie that He is not big enough to help me or cover my needs. He showed me that He is infinite and in control. He is able to cover me and everything in my life. God is big and God is love.”

JEANNETTE
Colorado

CHAPTER FIVE

ENCOUNTER ART WITH FATHER GOD

The first three Art Sozo activities in this book are centered around Father God who loves us, calls out our identity, protects us, and provides for us. We cannot comprehend the depth of Father God's great love for us!

Your identity is who He says you are. It is not about what you do in life, your job, your role in the home; it's about who you are and Whose you are.

He calls you His beloved child. He loved you and chose you before you knew Him, before you loved Him. You have always been loved. His protection and provision are built into His love for us. The word "beloved" is described in the dictionary as, "Dearly loved; adored; cherished; treasured, prized; highly favored; admired; esteemed."[1]

He is inviting you to experience His love as you paint through these activities. Open your heart and receive from Him.

"The Spirit Himself bears witness with our spirit that we are children of God...
heirs of God and joint heirs with Christ..."
Romans 8:16-17 (NKJV)

"Behold what manner of love the Father has bestowed on us,
that we should be called children of God!"
1 John 3:1 (NKJV)

1: Google Dictionary

FATHER GOD WHO GIVES US OUR IDENTITY AS HIS CHILDREN

"...you received God's Spirit when he adopted you as his own children. Now we call him, 'Abba, Father.'" Romans 8:15 (NLT)

Identity: "who a person is, or the qualities of a person or group, that makes them different from others."[2]

Father God wants to draw you close and have you fully receive and experience His love. In this art encounter you will connect to the heart of Father God and hear Him speak into your identity as His child.

ART SOZO ENCOUNTER ACTIVITY

Overview

While playing peaceful music, follow each step as you encounter Father God and listen for His voice of truth as you paint with Him.

Begin

Take a deep breath and relax.

Pray: "Father God, bring me deeper revelation of You as I paint today."

Ask: "Father God, what lie am I believing about my identity?" (Choose 2 colors and paint the lie onto the canvas.)

Ask: "Father God, who do I need to forgive for this lie? (Choose 2 colors and paint forgiveness onto the canvas.)

2: Cambridge Dictionary

Declare: "I forgive you for...(express in your own words) and the way it has affected my life. I release you from my judgement. Today, I say you owe me nothing, and I bless you."

Declare: "I renounce that this lie is true about me."

Ask: "Father God, what do You say is true about my identity?" (Choose 2 colors and paint what Father God says is true.)

Ask: "Father God, what else do you want me to know today?" (Choose 2 colors and paint what else Father God wants you to know today.)

Notes: Use the space below to take brief notes while painting.

Journal: Once your painting is complete, use the following two pages to journal what God revealed to you about your identity. When you finish journaling, make a copy and attach it to the back of your painting to help you remember what He spoke to you in this painting time.

JOURNAL

JOURNAL

FATHER GOD WHO PROTECTS US

"You are my hiding place; You shall preserve me from trouble; You shall surround me with songs of deliverance." Psalm 32:7 (NKJV)

Protector: "A person or thing that protects; defender; or guardian."[3]

Father God is your good, good Father who wants to assure you of His loving care and protection in your life. Allow Him to show you all the ways He protects you as you spend time in His presence today.

ART SOZO ENCOUNTER ACTIVITY

Overview
While playing peaceful music, follow each step as you encounter Father God and listen for His voice of truth as you paint with Him.

Begin
Take a deep breath and relax.

Pray: "Father God, bring me deeper revelation of You as I paint today."

Ask: "Father God, what lie am I believing about You and Your protection?" (Choose 2 colors and paint the lie onto the canvas.)

Ask: "Father God, who do I need to forgive for this lie?" (Choose 2 colors and paint forgiveness onto the canvas.)

3: Dictionary.com

Declare: "I forgive you for … (express in your own words) and the way it has affected my life. I release you from my judgement. Today I say you owe me nothing, and I bless you."

Declare: "I renounce that this lie is true about You, Father God."

Ask: "Father God, what is true about You and Your protection?" (Choose 2 colors and paint what Father God says is true.)

Ask: "Father God, how do You feel about me?" (Choose 2 colors and paint how Father God feels about you.)

Notes: Use the space below to take brief notes while painting.

Journal: Use the following pages to journal the truth Father God revealed to you about His heart of protection towards you. Make a copy and attach it to the back of your painting.

JOURNAL

JOURNAL

FATHER GOD WHO PROVIDES FOR US

"And my God shall supply all your need according to His riches in glory by Christ Jesus." Philippians 4:19 (NKJV)

Provider: "A person who gives someone something they need. Benefactor; helper; supplier."[4]

One of the best known names of God is Jehovah-Jireh, God the Provider. In Matthew 7:7, Jesus tells you to simply ask and it will be given to you. As you paint this encounter, let God reveal His desire to provide all that you need.

ART SOZO ENCOUNTER ACTIVITY

Overview

While playing peaceful music, follow each step as you encounter Father God and listen for His voice of truth as you paint with Him.

Begin

Take a deep breath and relax.

Pray: "Father God, bring me deeper revelation of You as I paint today."

Ask: "Father God, what lie am I believing about You and Your provision?" (Choose 2 colors and paint the lie onto the canvas.)

Ask: "Father God, who do I need to forgive for this lie?" (Choose 2 colors and paint forgiveness onto the canvas.)

4: Vocabulary.com

Declare: "I forgive you for … (express in your own words) and the way it has affected my life. I release you from my judgment. Today, I say you owe me nothing, and I bless you."

Declare: "I renounce that this lie is true about You, God."

Ask: "Father God, what is true about You and Your desire to provide for me?" (Choose 2 colors and paint what Father God says is true.)

Ask: "Father God, how do you see me?"
(Choose 2 colors and paint how Father God sees you.)

Notes: Use the space below to take brief notes while painting.

Journal: Use the following pages to journal the truth Father God revealed to you about His heart to provide for you. Make a copy and attach it to the back of your painting.

JOURNAL

JOURNAL

“

“I was believing I had to initiate my time spent with Jesus. I had to forgive the church for teaching me so much about works and performance. Jesus showed me how often throughout the day He gets my attention and it’s not just my thoughts, it is Him seeking me out as a companion.”

KARISSA
California

CHAPTER SIX

ENCOUNTER ART WITH JESUS

In the following three activities, you will be encountering Jesus as your Companion, Friend, and Savior.

Jesus wants to impart truth to you as you paint these art encounters with Him. He invites you into friendship, a deeper relationship of trust that allows you to pour out your heart and tell Him your hopes and dreams. Invite Him into every area of your life. He isn't distant or aloof. He is close, personal and enjoys spending time with you.

Like the apostle Paul, let your heart's cry be to know Jesus, to really know Him, as your own Savior, Companion and Friend. Nothing can compare to really knowing Jesus.

He is with you and He is for you. Jesus wants to speak to you more than you know.

"Greater love has no one than this, than to lay down one's life for his friends... No longer do I call you servants...I have called you friends, for all things that I heard from My Father I have made known to you."

John 15:13-15 (NKJV)

JESUS OUR COMPANION

"And be sure of this: I am with you always, even to the end of the age."
Matt 28:20 (NLT)

Companion: "A person you spend a lot of time with often because you are friends or because you are traveling together."[1]

As you paint, you will be connecting to Jesus as your Companion. Jesus wants to draw you close today and spend quality time with you. He is your constant Companion, the One who will never leave you or forsake you.

ART SOZO ENCOUNTER ACTIVITY

Overview
While playing peaceful music, follow each step as you encounter Jesus and listen for His voice of truth as you paint with Him.

Begin
Take a deep breath and relax.

Pray: "Jesus, bring me deeper revelation of You as I paint today."

Ask: "Jesus, what lie am I believing about You being my Companion?"(Choose 2 colors and paint the lie onto the canvas.)

Ask: "Jesus, who do I need to forgive for this lie?"
(Choose 2 colors and paint forgiveness onto the canvas.)

1: Cambridge Dictionary

Declare: "I forgive you for … (express in your own words) and the way it has affected my life. I release you from my judgement. Today, I say you owe me nothing, and I bless you."

Declare: "I renounce that this lie is true about You, Jesus."

Ask: "Jesus, what is true about You as my Companion?"
(Choose 2 colors and paint what Jesus says is true.)

Ask: "Jesus, how do You see me?"
(Choose 2 colors and paint how Jesus sees you.)

Notes: Use the space below to take brief notes while painting.

Journal: Use the following pages to journal what Jesus revealed to you about His heart to be your constant Companion. Make a copy and attach it to the back of your painting.

JOURNAL

JOURNAL

JESUS OUR FRIEND

"No longer do I call you servants...but I have called you friends..."
John 15:15 (NKJV)

Friend: "A person attached to another by feelings of affection or personal regard."[2]

A close friend is a person you feel comfortable with whether in silence or in conversation. Today, in the stillness, ask Jesus to draw close and wait for Him there. Allow time in this quiet place today to ask Jesus to reveal Himself to you as your Friend. He loves to spend time with you.

ART SOZO ENCOUNTER ACTIVITY

Overview
While playing peaceful music, follow each step as you encounter Jesus and listen for His voice of truth as you paint with Him.

Begin
Take a deep breath and relax.

Pray: "Jesus, bring me deeper revelation of You as I paint today."

Ask: "Jesus, what lie am I believing about You as my Friend?"
(Choose 2 colors and paint the lie onto the canvas.)

Ask: "Jesus, who do I need to forgive for this lie?"
(Choose 2 colors and paint forgiveness onto the canvas.)

2: Dictionary.com

Declare: "I forgive you for … (express in your own words) and the way it has affected my life. I release you from my judgement. Today, I say you owe me nothing, and I bless you."

Declare: "I renounce that this lie is true about You, Jesus."

Ask: "Jesus, what is true about You?"
(Choose 2 colors and paint what Jesus says is true.)

Ask: "Jesus how do You see me?"
(Choose 2 colors and paint how Jesus sees you.)

Notes: Use the space below to take brief notes while painting.

Journal: Use the following pages to journal what Jesus revealed to you as you painted about your friendship with Him. Make a copy and attach it to the back of your painting.

JOURNAL

JOURNAL

JESUS OUR SAVIOR

"And we have seen and testify that the Father has sent the Son as Savior of the world." 1 John 4:14 (NIV)

Savior: "One that saves from danger or destruction. One who brings salvation. A person that saves, rescues, or delivers."[3]

Jesus has saved your soul eternally. Let Him speak to you today of the deep revelation of your salvation in Him. Remember the finished work of the cross, all He accomplished for you there, and encounter Him as your personal Savior as you paint. Open your heart to Him and experience the joy of your salvation!

ART SOZO ENCOUNTER ACTIVITY

Overview
While playing peaceful music, follow each step as you encounter Jesus and listen for His voice of truth as you paint with Him.

Begin
Take a deep breath and relax.

Pray: "Jesus, bring me deeper revelation of You as I paint today."

Ask: "Jesus, what lie am I believing about You being my Savior?"
(Choose 2 colors and paint the lie onto the canvas.)

Ask: "Jesus who do I need to forgive for this lie?"
(Choose 2 colors and paint forgiveness onto the canvas.)

3: Merriam-Webster Dictionary

Declare: "I forgive you for … (express in your own words) and the way it has affected my life. I release you from my judgement. Today, I say you owe me nothing, and I bless you."

Declare: "I renounce that this lie is true about You, Jesus."

Ask: "Jesus, what is true about You?"
(Choose 2 colors and paint what Jesus says is true.)

Ask: "Jesus, how do You feel about me?"
(Choose 2 colors and paint how Jesus feels about you.)

Notes: Use the space below to take brief notes while painting.

Journal: Use the following pages to journal what Jesus revealed to you while you painted. Make a copy and attach it to the back of your painting.

JOURNAL

JOURNAL

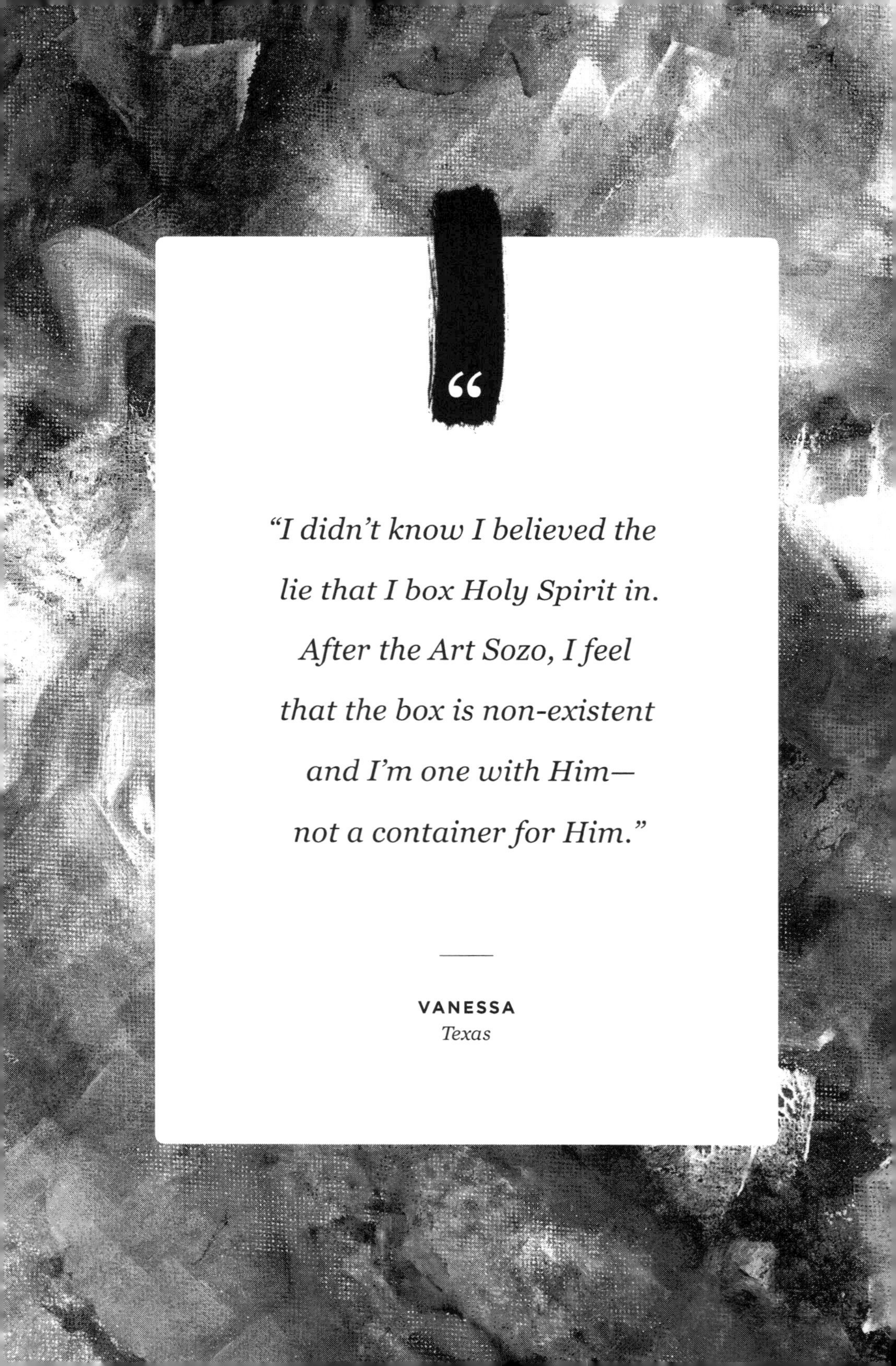

“

“I didn’t know I believed the lie that I box Holy Spirit in. After the Art Sozo, I feel that the box is non-existent and I’m one with Him— not a container for Him.”

VANESSA
Texas

CHAPTER SEVEN

ENCOUNTER ART WITH HOLY SPIRIT

In these activities, you will be encountering Holy Spirit as your Comforter, Nurturer, and Teacher. Holy Spirit is God within you. As you paint, allow Holy Spirit to draw you close and comfort you as only He can, speaking words of truth to you about His desire to nurture and teach you.

As you set time aside today, simply become aware of His presence within you and all around you. May you find freedom and the ability to connect to Him at a deeper level as you enjoy painting with Him, listening to His voice, and learning His ways.

He is wisdom and He is truth. He knows what to do in every situation you are facing. He knows what has gone before and what is ahead. He knows your innermost thoughts and feelings, and can help you through every trial and circumstance. He is God with you!

"And I will pray the Father, and He will give you another Helper, that He may abide with you forever—the Spirit of truth, whom the world cannot receive, because it neither sees Him nor knows Him; but you know Him, for He dwells with you and will be in you."
John 14:16-17 (NKJV)

"However, when He, the Spirit of truth, has come, He will guide you into all truth...and He will tell you things to come."
John 16:13 (NKJV)

HOLY SPIRIT OUR COMFORTER

"Nevertheless I tell you the truth; It is expedient for you that I go away: for if I go not away, the Comforter will not come to you; but if I depart, I will send him to you." John 16:7 (NRSV)

Comforter: "Someone who helps you feel less worried, upset or frightened, etc; someone who comforts you."[1]

Today, experience connecting to Holy Spirit as the Comforter. Allow Him to draw you close to His heart into deeper intimacy. Engage with Holy Spirit in each question, and let Him lead you into all truth about His heart to comfort and help you in every situation.

ART SOZO ENCOUNTER ACTIVITY

Overview
While playing peaceful music, follow each step as you encounter Holy Spirit and listen for His voice of truth as you paint.

Begin
Take a deep breath and relax.

Pray: "Holy Spirit, bring me deeper revelation of You as I paint today."

Ask: "Holy Spirit, what lie am I believing about being comforted by You?" (Choose 2 colors and paint the lie onto the canvas.)

1: Merriam-Webster's Dictionary

Ask: "Holy Spirit, who do I need to forgive for this lie?"
(Choose 2 colors and paint forgiveness onto the canvas.)

Declare: "I forgive you for ... (express in your own words) and the way it has affected my life. I release you from my judgement. Today, I say you owe me nothing, and I bless you."

Declare: "I renounce that this lie is true about You, Holy Spirit."

Ask: "Holy Spirit, what is true about You and Your comfort?"
(Choose 2 colors and paint what Holy Spirit says is true.)

Ask: "Holy Spirit, how do You feel about me?"
(Choose 2 colors and paint how Holy Spirit feels about you.)

Notes: Use the space below to take brief notes while painting.

Journal: Use the following pages to journal what Holy Spirit revealed while you painted about His desire to draw close and comfort you. Make a copy and attach it to the back of your painting.

JOURNAL

JOURNAL

HOLY SPIRIT OUR NURTURER

"Surely your goodness and unfailing love will pursue me all the days of my life, and I will live in the house of the LORD forever." Psalm 23:6 (NLT)

Nurture: "Care for and encourage the growth or development of."[2]

Holy Spirit desires to nurture you. Open your heart and mind to His voice with each question. Explore how He cares for you and encourages growth in your life. Allow Him to lead you to a deeper level of understanding and teach you about His love and care for you.

ART SOZO ENCOUNTER ACTIVITY

Overview

While playing peaceful music, follow each step as you encounter Holy Spirit and listen for His voice of truth as you paint with Him.

Begin

Take a deep breath and relax.

Pray: "Holy Spirit, bring me deeper revelation of You as I paint today."

Ask: "Holy Spirit, what lie am I believing about being nurtured by You?" (Choose 2 colors and paint the lie onto the canvas.)

Ask: "Holy Spirit, who do I need to forgive for this lie?" (Choose 2 colors and paint forgiveness onto the canvas.)

2: Oxford English Dictionary

Declare: "I forgive you for ...(express in your own words) and the way it has affected my life. I release you from my judgement. Today, I say you owe me nothing, and I bless you."

Declare: "I renounce that this lie is true about You, Holy Spirit."

Ask: "Holy Spirit, what is true about You?"
(Choose 2 colors and paint what Holy Spirit says is true.)

Ask: "Holy Spirit, how do You see me?"
(Choose 2 colors and paint how Holy Spirit sees you.)

Notes: Use the space below to take brief notes while painting.

Journal: Use the following pages to journal what Holy Spirit revealed to you while you painted. Make a copy and attach it to the back of your painting.

JOURNAL

JOURNAL

HOLY SPIRIT OUR TEACHER

"But the Helper, the Holy Spirit, whom the Father will send in My name, He will teach you all things, and bring to your remembrance all things that I said to you." John 14:26 (NKJV)

Teach: "Impart knowledge to or instruct someone as to how to do something."[3]

One of the facets of Holy Spirit is Teacher. He lives inside you and is committed to helping you understand the Bible and the ways of the Kingdom. From before the world was formed, He has always been the greatest and wisest Teacher! Invite Holy Spirit to show you the deep truths about His nature. Receive insight and revelation from Him as you paint.

ART SOZO ENCOUNTER ACTIVITY

Overview
While playing peaceful music, follow each step as you encounter Holy Spirit and listen for His voice of truth as you paint with Him.

Begin
Take a deep breath and relax.

Pray: "Holy Spirit, bring me deeper revelation of You as I paint today."

Ask: "Holy Spirit, what lie am I believing about You being my Teacher?" (Choose 2 colors and paint the lie onto the canvas.)

3: Oxford English Dictionary

Ask: "Holy Spirit, who do I need to forgive for this lie?"
(Choose 2 colors and paint forgiveness onto the canvas.)

Declare: "I forgive you for ... (express in your own words) and the way it has affected my life. I release you from my judgement. Today, I say you owe me nothing, and I bless you."

Declare: "I renounce that this lie is true about You, Holy Spirit."

Ask: "Holy Spirit, what is true about You?"
(Choose 2 colors and paint what Holy Spirit says is true.)

Ask: "Holy Spirit, what do You think about me?"
(Choose 2 colors and paint what Holy Spirit thinks about you.)

Notes: Use the space below to take brief notes while painting.

Journal: Use the following pages to journal the truth Holy Spirit revealed to you while you painted. Make a copy and attach it to the back of your painting.

JOURNAL

JOURNAL

"

"God has been speaking to me about moving beyond having faith that He is able, but that He also is good and trusting that part with my heart. This exercise moved me from seeing Him as just a distant God who wants good things for me to an involved God who wants to partner with and journey with me, and to be fully involved."

ROWENA
California

CHAPTER EIGHT

MORE ENCOUNTER ART WITH GOD

By now, you have completed the first nine activities and have encountered Father God, Jesus, and Holy Spirit in fresh new ways. These activities have laid a foundation before continuing on to the following encounters by letting God heal many areas where you may have had wounds or lies. At any time, you can go back and encounter Him again in the first nine activities and He will reveal new things to you about His nature and how He sees you.

The following activities are designed to help you go deeper in your experience with God in the areas of authenticity, rest, worship, the desires of your heart and dreaming with Him. As you paint through these Art Sozo activities with God, your relationship with Him will deepen, leading you into greater connection and intimacy. God is committed to completing the good work He has started in you. He is faithful!

"Deep calls to deep at the sound of Your waterfalls; all Your breakers and Your waves have rolled over me."
Psalm 42:7 (NASB)

"Draw near to God and He will draw near to you."
James 4:8 (NASB)

AUTHENTICITY BEFORE GOD

"Jesus saw Nathanael coming toward Him, and said of him, 'Behold, an Israelite indeed, in whom is no deceit!'" John 1:47 (NKJV)

Authentic: "Of undisputed origin and not a copy; genuine."[1]

Jesus knows our hearts; there is nothing hidden from Him. What a joy to be fully known and fully loved! Being authentic before God and people is the only way to live a joyful, honest, and fulfilled life.

ART SOZO ENCOUNTER ACTIVITY

Overview

While playing peaceful music, follow each step as you encounter Jesus and listen for His voice of truth as you paint with Him.

Begin

Take a deep breath and relax.

Pray: "Jesus, bring me deeper revelation of You as I paint with You today."

Ask: "Jesus, what lie am I believing about being authentic?" (Choose 2 colors and paint the lie onto the canvas.)

Ask: "Jesus, who do I need to forgive for this lie?" (Choose 2 colors and paint forgiveness onto the canvas.)

1: Oxford English Dictionary

Declare: "I forgive you…(express in your own words) and the way it has affected my life. I release you from my judgement. Today, I say you owe me nothing, and I bless you."

Declare: "I renounce that this lie is true."

Ask: "Jesus, what is true about You and authenticity?"
(Choose 2 colors and paint what Jesus says is true.)

Ask: "Jesus, how do You see me and feel about me?"
(Choose 2 colors and paint how Jesus sees and feels about you.)

Notes: Use the space below to take brief notes while painting.

Journal: Use the following pages to journal the truth Jesus revealed to you about being authentic. Make a copy and attach it to the back of your painting.

JOURNAL

JOURNAL

REST

"The Lord is my Shepherd; I shall not want. He makes me to lie down in green pastures; He leads me beside the still waters. He restores my soul."
Psalm 23:1-3 (NKJV)

Rest: "To cease work or movement in order to relax, sleep, or recover strength. Allow to be inactive in order to regain strength or health."[2]

Take time to rest in His presence, breathe Him in, and renew your strength in the secret place. How does it feel to rest in Him? Picture yourself by the still waters, lying in the green pasture with the sun on your face. Let Him restore you and give you His strength.

ART SOZO ENCOUNTER ACTIVITY

Overview
While playing peaceful music, follow each step as you encounter Holy Spirit and listen for His voice of truth as you paint.

Begin
Take a deep breath and relax.

Pray: "Holy Spirit, bring me deeper revelation of You as I paint today."

Ask: "Holy Spirit, what lie am I believing about entering Your rest each day?" (Choose 2 colors and paint the lie onto the canvas.)

2: Oxford English Dictionary

Ask: "Holy Spirit, who do I need to forgive for this lie?" (Choose 2 colors and paint forgiveness onto the canvas.)

Declare: "I forgive you for … (express in your own words) and the way it has affected my life. I release you from my judgement. Today, I say you owe me nothing, and I bless you."

Declare: "I renounce that this lie is true about You, Holy Spirit."

Ask: "Holy Spirit, what is true about You?" (Choose 2 colors and paint what Holy Spirit says is true.)

Ask: "Holy Spirit, what do You think about me?" (Choose 2 colors and paint what Holy Spirit thinks about you.)

Notes: Use the space below to take brief notes while painting.

Journal: Use the following pages to journal the truth Holy Spirit revealed to you about rest. Make a copy and attach it to the back of your painting.

JOURNAL

JOURNAL

WORSHIP

"But the hour is coming, and now is, when the true worshipers will worship the Father in spirit and truth; for the Father is seeking such to worship Him. God is Spirit, and those who worship Him must worship in spirit and truth."
John 4: 23-24 (NKJV)

Worship: "Worship is the submission of all our nature to God. It is the quickening of conscience by His holiness; the nourishment of mind by His truth; the purifying of imagination by His beauty; the opening of the heart to His love; the surrender of will to His purpose—and all of this gathered up in adoration…"[3]

Before you start to paint today, worship the Lord with all your heart. Thank Him for His goodness in your life, and remember His kindness to you. Let worship spring up from within you—you were created to worship Him! Ask God to reveal to you what it means to worship Him in spirit and truth. Let Him speak to you about true worship from the heart.

ART SOZO ENCOUNTER ACTIVITY

Overview
While playing peaceful music, follow each step as you encounter Father God and listen for His voice of truth as you paint.

Begin
Take a deep breath and relax.

Pray: "Father God, bring me deeper revelation of You as I paint today."

3: Theopedia

Reflect: What does worship look and feel like to you? (Choose two colors and paint how worship looks and feels onto the canvas.)

Ask: "God, how do You feel about worship?" (Choose two colors and paint how God feels about worship onto the canvas.)

Continue to stay in the emotion of how God feels about worship and let Him encounter you as you paint. (Use any colors to paint your encounter with God.)

Notes: Use the space below to take brief notes while painting.

Journal: Use the following pages to journal the truth Father God revealed to you about worship. Make a copy and attach it to the back of your painting.

JOURNAL

JOURNAL

DESIRES OF YOUR HEART

"Delight yourself also in the Lord, and He shall give you the desires of your heart."
Psalm 37:4 (NKJV)

Desire: "A strong feeling of wanting to have something or wishing for something to happen."[4]

Draw close to God in a quiet place, delight in Him, and enjoy His presence for a few moments. Talk to Him about the desires of your heart, and pour out the longings of your heart to Him, because He cares deeply for you. Often, the desires of your heart were placed there by Father God Himself so that He can bless you and fulfill those desires as you delight yourself in Him.

ART SOZO ENCOUNTER ACTIVITY

Overview
While playing peaceful music, follow each step as you encounter Father God and listen for His voice of truth as you paint with him. From a place of trust and peace, ask God to remind you of the deepest desires of your heart.

Begin
Take a deep breath and relax.

Pray: "Father God, please show me more of Your loving ways as I paint today."

Ask: "God, is there a lie I am believing about Your promise to bless me with the desires of my heart?" (Choose 2 colors and paint the lie He shows you onto the canvas.)

4: Oxford English Dictionary

Ask: "Father God, who do I need to forgive for this lie?" (Choose 2 colors and paint forgiveness onto the canvas.)

Declare: "I forgive you for…(express in your own words) and the way it has affected my life. I release you from my judgement. Today, I say you owe me nothing and I bless you."

Declare: "I renounce that this lie is true."

Ask: "Father God, what is true about Your promise to bless me with the desires of my heart?" (Choose 2 colors and paint what God says is true.)

Ask: "Father God, how do You see me and feel about me?" (Choose 2 colors and paint how God sees you and feels about you.)

Notes: Write down what God shows you as you paint, then spend some time journaling as you focus on the truth He has revealed to you.

Journal: Use the following pages to journal the truth Father God revealed to you about the desires of your heart. Make a copy and attach it to the back of your painting.

JOURNAL

JOURNAL

DREAMING WITH GOD

"For nothing is impossible with God." Luke 1:37 (NLT)

Dreaming with God:

"God starts to build your faith by giving you a dream...that dream you have, the idea or concept you've been thinking about doing that would be of real benefit to other people..." - Rick Warren, Senior Pastor at Saddleback Church[5]

Daring to dream again with God, knowing He is a good, good Father, is of vital importance in order to hope again. He has placed His dreams and desires for your life in your heart so that He can fulfill them. What would it look like to allow Him to stir up hope for those dreams and desires and to step out in faith, believing that He cares deeply about your heart?

"You are God's idea, and He longs to see the treasure that is in your heart. As we learn to dream with God we become co-laborers with Him."
- Bill Johnson, Senior leader at Bethel Church[6]

ART SOZO ENCOUNTER ACTIVITY

Overview

While playing peaceful music, follow each step as you encounter God and listen for His voice of truth as you paint.

Begin

Take a deep breath and relax.

5: Quoted from his May 2014 article, "God Gives You A Dream To Build Your Faith," on PastorRick.com.

6: Quoted from Dreaming With God: Co-laboring With God for Cultural Transformation by Bill Johnson.

Pray: "Father God, bring me deeper revelation of You and the dreams You've placed in my heart as I paint with You today."

Ask: "Father God, is there a lie I am believing about dreaming with You?" (Choose 2 colors and paint the lie He shows you onto the canvas.)

Ask: "Father God, who do I need to forgive for this lie?" (Choose 2 colors and paint forgiveness onto the canvas.)

Declare: "I forgive you...(express in your own words) and the way it has affected my life. I release you from my judgement. Today, I say you owe me nothing, and I bless you."

Declare: "I renounce that this lie is true."

Ask: "Father God, what is true about dreaming with you?" (Choose 2 colors and paint what He says is true about Himself.)

Ask: "Father God, what do You say about the dreams that are in my heart?" (Choose 2 colors and paint what He shows you onto your canvas.)

Notes: Use the space below to take brief notes while painting.

Journal: Use the following pages to journal the truth Father God revealed to you about dreaming with Him. Make a copy and attach it to the back of your painting.

JOURNAL

JOURNAL

"I was able to identify a lie that I'm not enough and forgive those from my past that spoke that over me. I now know that I'm more than enough and that Christ in me has equipped me to do what I once thought was impossible."

APRIL
California

CHAPTER NINE

CONTINUING THE JOURNEY

While writing this book, I reviewed many of the paintings I've done throughout the years and I found it so encouraging to see the journey I've been on with God. After feeling like a victim, not having a voice, and not feeling like I was enough for most of my life, Father God lovingly restored my identity and called me to write this book to carry His message of healing to others.

You have been on your own journey of encounter art with God and as He lovingly speaks truth into the areas of your life the enemy has tried to steal, I am excited for how you will be walking out the destiny He has for you in a more clear, purposeful way. I encourage you to review your paintings and journaling and let God continue to minister to you through them. Stewarding what He has done in the painting times will keep these messages of truth alive.

I also encourage you to keep painting and processing with God, even going back through this book and painting through the same exercises. No matter how many times you paint through the same prompts, God will lead you through new encounters and revelation. He has so much He wants to reveal to you as you put yourself in the way of encounters with Him!

Thank you for entrusting your heart to the Art Sozo process. I pray that God seals the good work He has done and binds the truths He has revealed to you in your heart. I bless you on your Art Sozo journey as you paint and pursue intimacy with God.

Gail

REFERENCES

Cambridge Dictionary. Last modified 2017. http://dictionary.cambridge.org

De Silva, Dawna, and Teresa Liebscher. Sozo Basic Training Manual. Redding: Bethel, 2011.

Dictionary.com. Last modified 2017. http://www.dictionary.com

Google Dictionary. Last accessed August 2017. https://www.google.com/search?q=google+dictionary&oq=google+dictionary+&aqs=chrome..69i57j0l5.7655j0j4&sourceid=chrome&ie=UTF-8#dobs=beloved

Johnson, Bill. Dreaming With God: Co-laboring With God for Cultural Transformation. Shippensburg: Destiny Image, 2006.

"Lexicon: Strong's G4982 - sōzō." August 19, 2017. Blue Letter Bible. https://www.blueletterbible.org/lang/lexicon/lexicon.cfm?t=nasb&strongs=g4982.

Merriam-Webster Dictionary. Last modified 2017. https://www.merriam-webster.com

Oxford English Dictionary. Last modified 2017. http://www.oed.com

Theopedia. Last accessed August 2017. http://www.theopedia.com/worship.

Vocabulary.com. Last accessed August 2017. https://www.vocabulary.com/dictionary/provider.

Warren, Rick. "God Gives You A Dream To Build Your Faith." May 21, 2014. Pastor Rick's Daily Hope. http://pastorrick.com/devotional/english/god-gives-you-a-dream-to-build-your-faith

WordReference.com. Last accessed August 2017. http://www.wordreference.com/

YourDictionary.com. Last accessed August 2017. http://www.yourdictionary.com/

Zaigon, Laurie. "The 4 Emotions." Training handout, Art4Healing Certification Course, Laguna Hills, CA, 2011.

APPENDIX A

COMMON QUESTIONS

In these activities, you will be asking God questions such as, "Is there a lie I am believing about you, God?" or "What is Your truth about this topic?" and responding to the truth He shows you through painting. Here are some common questions that come up when painting with God in this way.

What if I can't hear God's response?

It is God's heart that we live in perfect union with Him, and there can be no union without communication. Jeremiah 33:3 says, "Call to Me and I will answer you, and will tell you great and hidden things that you have not known" (NASB).

As you paint, you are calling on Him to answer you in this process, and He promises He will. You were created to hear from God, but keep in mind that His responses may not come how you expect. God can speak to us directly in His "...still small voice" (1 Kings 19:12 ASV). He also speaks using images, Bible verses, impressions, senses, or just an inner knowing. Whatever comes up as you ask Him questions, be it a color, an image, or a thought that may not even make sense to you in the moment, just keep painting. Trust that whatever you sense or hear while painting is something God is speaking. You will be amazed by what He can tell you as you trust that He is with you in the process and really wants to speak to you.

How could I believe a lie about God?

God and His truth are constant, but sometimes things happen in our lives that keep us from seeing Him clearly. Here's an example: look at something in your view right now that you enjoy seeing. Now, as you continue looking at that object or scene, put your hands up in front of your face with your fingers spread wide. The object you were looking at hasn't changed. What is true about it hasn't changed. But you're not able to see it clearly or as a whole because your fingers are obstructing your view. Your fingers have, in effect, distorted how you see. Lies can be like those fingers, as they prevent you from seeing God as He really is.

Wounds and lies can become filters through which we see God. It could be as simple as a comment made by a classmate in elementary school that made you feel rejected, or something more complicated like a trauma that brought shame into your life. A past wound or lie can lead you to think or feel something that is contrary to what the Bible says is true about your identity or God's truth. This lie clouds your view of God and hinders a complete heart connection with Him. What filters in your life are you viewing God through? He is eagerly waiting to meet you right where you are and restore your belief system to align with His truth by removing these filters.

How can I tell if something is God's truth or mine?

If it's biblical, it's God. If not, you may have uncovered a lie or wound that will need a little more time to process. If what you are hearing or sensing while you paint feels judgemental, harsh, or punitive, it is not God's truth, but possibly lies from being wounded. If you feel hesitation, ask God what He thinks about it. He's right there with you, always.

What if I'm not ready to forgive someone?

Did anything come up when you were invited to "forgive?" When an activity calls for forgiveness, it is not saying what happened was okay or asking you to forget all about it. Forgiveness is not validating an action or allowing it to happen again. Forgiveness is handing the person and hurt over to Jesus and letting Him handle it instead. Forgiving is a choice not to carry it around anymore and to let Him bring His justice and resolve. Forgiveness ushers in freedom for your heart.

APPENDIX B

ART SOZO WORKSHOPS

The Art Sozo Workshop was founded by Gail Spooner in 2013. It is a combination of Bethel Sozo inner healing tools and "encounter art," with the goal of connecting participants to their emotions and to the heart of God. Thousands of participants have been led through the three-hour group workshops and have encountered God in a unique and fresh new way. This activity book is designed to give individuals an opportunity to experience the Art Sozo process on their own at home and for participants of the Art Sozo Workshop to continue their Art Sozo healing journey. If you enjoyed the process, you'll love connecting with others in one of these unique art workshop encounters. Go to *artsozo.com* for more information on the Art Sozo Workshop and the Art Sozo Leader Training.

TESTIMONIES FROM ART SOZO WORKSHOPS:

"It was a really beautiful and gentle experience. It felt very safe and comfortable, and I loved being led through the different exercises and seeing what I created. I realized that I can see and feel things as I paint, and that God can talk to me and bring revelation in new ways! I'm keen to explore all of this further."

ANONYMOUS, UNITED KINGDOM

"I came in feeling very heavy in my heart. I felt a deep freedom in my spirit and saw and experienced God in a new way. He's so gracious to me! Very emotional."

LYNN, CALIFORNIA

"The process of Art Sozo, especially the Signature piece was such a powerful tool to experience intimacy with God in a new way."

SHANNON, CANADA

"I've felt like 'too much' my whole life. My mom (who is made the same way) was fearful I'd get hurt like she did, so she wanted to 'contain' me to protect me. I forgave her. I had to use lots of paint and lots of supplies and keep asking for more because God wants me to know He's enough and I can be all of me."

JENNIFER, IDAHO

"I came in not knowing what to expect and afraid to paint. The steps were great as I saw that I was holding a grudge... He walked me through forgiveness and I'm in His heart."

JOHNNY, COLORADO

"I really loved that my piece was not criticized. I appreciated that there were other 'non-artists' at the table. I was crying a lot throughout the painting. It touched me deeply."

KARA, COLORADO

"I prayed before I walked into the room, 'Lord, what do I need to hear?' I'm struggling with releasing the debt of pain… This Sozo showed me I could let go, I could release all the pain, God would be right there, protecting me, guiding me and reminding me to lean on Him—no matter what. I leave here longing to stay in His presence more and longer."

AIDA, IDAHO

"I was amazed how God showed up. I came in with low expectations and was more here for my wife but I found out it is easy to hear from God. He spoke clearly some confirming truths I really needed to hear."

ERIC, CALIFORNIA

"I was amazed on why I saw this strange picture. As I followed the steps, God's will was being revealed layer by layer. I sensed God's presence, and I felt grateful. I am also thrilled that I could take home my beautiful paintings."

CONNIE, CHINA

"This class probably saved my life. I was so heart broken by my abusive father and fiancé walking out on me and I was pleading to God but not hearing His voice. This workshop helped me forgive those people and by doing so, I could hear God once again. I know He will never walk out on me."

REBEKAH, IDAHO

APPENDIX C

VERSES ABOUT THE NATURE OF GOD

FATHER GOD

Our Identity

"God created man in His own image, in the image of God He created him; male and female He created them."

GENESIS 1:27 (NASB)

"For we are God's masterpiece. He has created us anew in Christ Jesus, so we can do the good things he planned for us long ago."

EPHESIANS 2:10 (NLT)

"But you are a chosen people, a royal priesthood, a holy nation, God's special possession, that you may declare the praises of him who called you out of darkness into his wonderful light."

1 PETER 2:9 (NIV)

"See what great love the Father has lavished on us, that we should be called children of God! And that is what we are! The reason the world does not know us is that it did not know him. Dear friends, now we are children of God, and what we will be has not yet been made known. But we know that when Christ appears, we shall be like him, for we shall see him as he is."

1 JOHN 3:1-2 (NIV)

Our Protection

"Many are the afflictions of the righteous, But the LORD delivers him out of them all."

PSALM 34:19 (NASB)

"So do not fear, for I am with you; do not be dismayed, for I am your God. I will strengthen you and help you; I will uphold you with my righteous right hand."

ISAIAH 41:10 (NIV)

"The LORD is good, A stronghold in the day of trouble, And He knows those who take refuge in Him."

NAHUM 1:7 (NASB)

"But the Lord is faithful, and He will strengthen and protect you from the evil one."

2 THESSALONIANS 3:3 (NASB)

Our Provision

"Look at the birds of the air, that they do not sow, nor reap nor gather into barns, and yet your heavenly Father feeds them. Are you not worth much more than they?"

MATTHEW 6:26 (NIV)

"Do not worry then, saying, 'What will we eat?' or 'What will we drink?' or 'What will we wear for clothing?' For the Gentiles eagerly seek all these things; for your heavenly Father knows that you need all these things. But seek first His kingdom and His righteousness, and all these things will be added to you."

MATTHEW 6:31-33 (NASB)

JESUS

Our Companion

"...Never will I leave you; never will I forsake you."

HEBREWS 13:5 (NIV)

"Behold, I stand at the door and knock; if anyone hears My voice and opens the door, I will come in to him and will dine with him, and he with Me."

REVELATION 3:20 (NASB)

Our Friend

"...But there is a friend who sticks closer than a brother."

PROVERBS 18:24 (NASB)

"Greater love has no one than this, that one lay down his life for his friends."

JOHN 15:13 (NASB)

Our Savior

"But he was pierced for our rebellion, crushed for our sins. He was beaten so we could be whole. He was whipped so we could be healed."

ISAIAH 53:5 (NLT)

"For the Son of Man came to seek and save those who are lost."

LUKE 19:10 (NLT)

"And there is salvation in no one else; for there is no other name under heaven that has been given among men by which we must be saved."

ACTS 4:12 (NASB)

"But God demonstrates his own love for us in this:
While we were still sinners, Christ died for us."

ROMANS 5:8 (NIV)

HOLY SPIRIT

Our Teacher

"I have filled him with the Spirit of God in
wisdom, in understanding, in knowledge, and in
all kinds of craftsmanship..."

EXODUS 31:3 (NASB)

"But I will send you the Advocate—the Spirit of truth.
He will come to you from the Father and will testify all about me."

JOHN 15:26 (NLT)

"All of them were filled with the Holy Spirit and began
to speak in other tongues as the Spirit enabled them."

ACTS 2:4 (NIV)

"And the Holy Spirit helps us in our weakness.
For example, we don't know what God wants us to
pray for. But the Holy Spirit prays for us with
groanings that cannot be expressed in words."

ROMANS 8:26 (NLT)

Our Nurturer

"But you, dear friends, by building yourselves up in your
most holy faith and praying in the Holy Spirit."

JUDE 1:20 (NIV)

"For this reason I remind you to fan into flame the gift of God, which is in you through the laying on of my hands. For the Spirit God gave us does not make us timid, but gives us power, love and self-discipline."

2 TIMOTHY 1:6-7 (NIV)

Our Comforter

"Nevertheless I tell you the truth; It is expedient for you that I go away: for if I go not away, the Comforter will not come to you; but if I depart, I will send him to you."

JOHN 16:7 (ASV)

APPENDIX D

A NOTE ON JOURNALING

While painting, sometimes it helps to make brief notes to remind yourself of your process for when you journal later. The reason for keeping it brief is because you want to stay in your "emotional brain" and out of the logical "words center" during these encounters. There is space at the end of each activity for you to jot these brief notes down. After you've finished painting, you can use the two blank pages following the activity to journal a more complete explanation of your experience. Make a copy of this and attach it to the back of your painting for future reference.

When journaling, ask God what He wants you to remember about the painting. He often wants to highlight the truth He's revealed to you during your encounter art time with Him. If it feels important to you to note what the lie was and who you forgave, I suggest you fold the copy of your journaling page, so when you tape it to the back of your painting, the lie will be facing in and be covered up, just like the lie has been covered up with the truth on your painting. In this way you can reference it, if needed, but as you go back and review your painting and all God has shown you is true on a regular basis, you will not be going back to old wounds and lies.

I encourage you to make time to write and reflect. View the journaling time as just as important as the painting time of your encounter with God. Sit with your painting and let Him continue to speak to you. He will often add to the meaning of the piece as you continue to listen and give you more clarity and revelation as you journal.

Some of our team members have found that if they don't have time to paint, they can write and journal through the activity prompts and have an encounter with God. Use this book however best fits your time and temperament, giving God space to encounter you.

APPENDIX E

RECOMMENDED RESOURCES

SUPPLIES

- **Dick Blick Art Supplies:** www.dickblick.com
- **Michaels Stores:** www.michaels.com
- **Motsenbocker's LIFT OFF** (Acrylic Paint Remover)

MUSIC

- **Justin Byrne - *Dreaming in Color***
  Available on Apple iTunes or at shop.bethel.com
- **Justin Byrne - *The Rest of Life***
  Available on Apple iTunes or at shop.bethel.com
- **Jan A.P. Kaczmarek - *Finding Neverland (Soundtrack from the Motion Picture)*** Available on Apple iTunes
- **Jay Stocker - *Quietly (A Piano Album), Vol. 1***
  Available on Apple iTunes
- **Bethel Music - *Without Words***
  Available on Apple iTunes or at shop.bethel.com
- **Bethel Music - *Without Words: Synesthesia***
  Available on Apple iTunes or at shop.bethel.com

FURTHER LEARNING

- *Art Sozo: Connecting to the Heart of God Through Art* by Gail Spooner. http://www.artsozo.com/store/art-sozo-training-manual
- *Sozo: Saved, Healed, Delivered - A Journey Into Freedom...* by Dawna De Silva & Teresa Liebscher. https://shop.bethel.com/products/sozo-saved-healed-delivered-a-journey-into-freedom-with-the-father-son-and-holy-spirit
- *Sozo Basic Training Manual* by Dawna De Silva & Teresa Liebscher. https://shop.bethel.com/products/sozo-basic-training-manual
- Art & Creativity for Healing Inc. - The Art4Healing® programs by Laurie Zaigon are based on Judeo-Christian values but do not specifically have a Christian focus. Attending the Art for Healing Certificate Program through Brandman University - Chapman University System was instrumental in Gail developing Art Sozo. *www.art4healing.org*

APPENDIX F

BETHEL SOZO

Bethel Sozo is an inner healing ministry developed in 1997 by Dawna DeSilva and Teresa Liebscher. It is named after the Greek word "Sozo" used over a hundred times in the New Testament, usually in reference to Jesus' miraculous work to holistically save, heal, and deliver those who receive Him. For instance, when the word "Sozo" is used in Acts 2:21, Strong's Concordance translates it as "save," "make whole," "heal," and "be whole." "But everyone who calls on the name of the LORD will be saved" (Acts 2:21 NLT).

Traditional Bethel Sozo sessions are designed to be an encounter with God during which counselors follow Holy Spirit to guide participants into greater freedom and revelation. The goal of each session is to connect the participant to the Godhead. This is done by identifying any wounds or lies that may be clouding a participant's ability to see God and fully experience His love and power. Under Holy Spirit's guidance, counselors use Sozo inner healing tools to help participants identify the original wound, forgive all those who are responsible for the wounding, renounce any lies they themselves may have believed, and ask God to replace the lies with His truth. It is a powerful process because Holy Spirit is able to reveal the core issue to the counselors and participants quickly.

Additional information about Bethel Sozo Ministry and how to schedule an appointment on Skype or with a counselor near you can be found online at: *www.bethelsozo.com/sozo-network*.

You may also contact the Sozo Ministry of Bethel Church directly:

Bethel Transformation Center
20 Lake Blvd.
Redding, CA 96003

Email: transformationcenter@ibethel.org
Phone: 530-229-7909
Website: bethelsozo.com

APPENDIX G

PAINT PLATE DIAGRAM

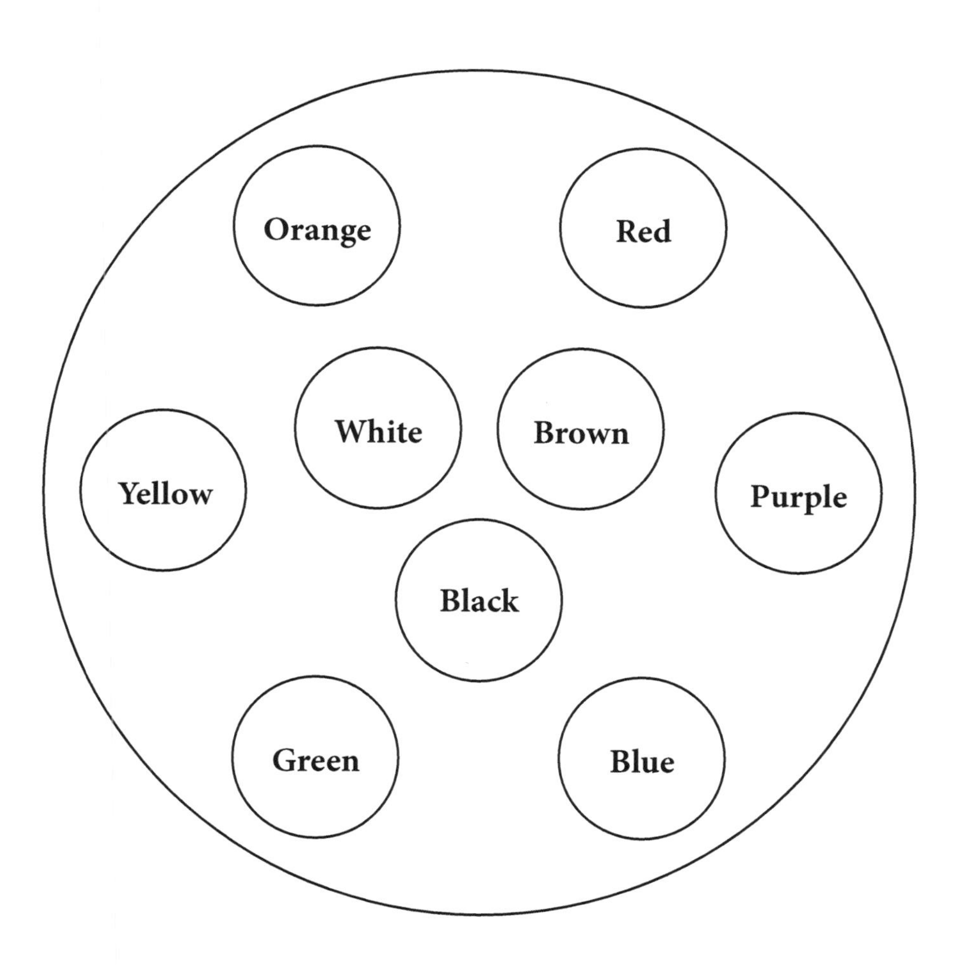

APPENDIX H

SUGGESTIONS FOR USE IN GROUP AND COUNSELING SETTINGS

Using *Art Sozo: Painting with God* as a small group curriculum:

- If you would like to go through these activities as a small group experience, I suggest limiting your group size to six or less participants. After you do an activity, each participant can share what God has shown them with the group. Since each person has *painted their heart* onto the canvas, I suggest not commenting, but just listening and giving them a safe place to share without evaluation. It may be fun to meet and paint through an exercise each week together, or you may choose to paint at home and meet once a week to share what you painted and what God showed you. When we use these activities in a group setting, we like to start our group time sharing testimonies of what God has revealed and healed and how it has played out in the participants' lives. It's amazing to see what God does in activating a new belief in everyday life.

Using *Art Sozo: Painting with God* for professional clinicians or Sozo counselors:

- Consider facilitating this material as an encounter group. Have clients experience the painting sessions together, and share what God has shown them in the small group. Follow up with individuals as you feel necessary using what they paint in the group as a way to go deeper in their regular sessions with you.
- If you are a trained Sozo Counselor, you may want to consider being trained in leading the Art Sozo Workshop. See *www.artsozo.com* for more information on the *Art Sozo Workshop Manual* and training locations.

GET CONNECTED

JOIN THE COMMUNITY

See art, read testimonies, and interact with others on the Art Sozo journey at *www.facebook.com/artsozo*

STAY INFORMED

Gail regularly holds workshops, leader trainings, and retreats at the Bethel Transformation Center in Redding, California and other parts of the world. If you are interested in attending, or would just like more information about the ministry, please visit *www.artsozo.com.*

Want to host an Art Sozo workshop, training, or retreat?
Invite Gail to visit your organization!
Submit inquiries at: *www.artsozo.com/contact.*

CONTACT GAIL

gail@artsozo.com

ABOUT THE AUTHOR

GAIL SPOONER

Gail Spooner is an author and trainer who loves to bring personal encounters with God to others. She is also a commissioned pastor with Bethel Church serving in the Transformation Center as a Sozo Counselor. Her passion for bringing freedom and connection to God, through art, led her to create the Art Sozo Workshop. Gail's background in counseling and therapeutic recreation, as well as certification as an Art4Healing facilitator through Chapman University, have uniquely equipped her to develop the Art Sozo process. While attending Bethel School of Supernatural Ministry, she was given the prophetic word: "You will raise up an army of artists who will heal the hearts of the world," and she enjoys seeing this prophecy come true! She lives in Redding, California, with her amazing husband Eli.

CONTRIBUTOR

Gillian Kingsley

Gillian and her husband Steve moved from England to Redding, California with a hunger to experience more of God, and to be part of Bethel Church. She attended Bethel School of Supernatural Ministry for the next three years, with her final year as Gail Spooner's intern in the Art Sozo ministry.

During this internship Gillian's passion for inner healing was stirred as she witnessed God bring healing to people's lives through art in the Art Sozo Workshops. She was awakened to "encounter art" and loves to lead the workshops to see others released into creativity and healing.

Made in the USA
Columbia, SC
19 November 2017